HOW TO KEEP THE DEVIL
off OF YOUR GUEST *List*

A Practical Guide for
Planning Christian Weddings

By
Kim Bush Mack

Edited by Dr. Sir Walter Mack, Jr.

All Scripture quotations are taken from the *King James Version* of the Bible.

How to Keep the Devil Off of Your Guest List: Grooms' Edition
A Practical Guide for Planning Christian Weddings
ISBN: 978-1-936314-68-3
Copyright © 2011 by Kim Bush Mack.

Published by Word and Spirit Resources
P.O. Box 701403
Tulsa, Oklahoma 74170

Acknowledgements

God is so awesome!!! On May 21, 2011, God allowed me to marry the most incredible man I could ever imagine as a husband. Six months later, I've now written my first book about the journey and planning of the worship service to celebrate our union. I could not complete this first project without acknowledging and thanking some very special people who have poured into me my entire life!

First to my church family, First Baptist Church, Apple Street, Burlington, North Carolina, and the Rev. Richard Styles and Rev. Helen Styles. You all helped raise me and ensured I had the Christian foundation I needed to become the person I am today. For that, I will be eternally grateful.

To my family, my parents, Erma Wilson Bush and the late Herbert Bush, my grandmother, the late Mable Wilson, my siblings, Ricky (Brenda), Rhonda (Sam), Ann (Gabe), Carl (Judy), Linda, Yvette (Eugene), Thomas (Sheila) and Wendy. You all are the best family a girl could have. You have always supported everything I have done and I love you all to the fullest. To all of my nieces, nephews, aunts, uncles and cousins...thank you for being that strong extended family I need all my life.

To my new family—the Mack family. What a wonderful set of "in-laws" to have. Since we met back in the late 80's, you all have been the same to me as my biological family...loving, caring and supportive. Thank you for your warm welcome of not only me, but for welcoming my entire family into your family.

To my new church family, the Union Baptist Church of Winston-Salem, North Carolina. You all have loved on me, honored me and respected me since the very beginning. I want you to know I don't take it for granted. I give you my heartfelt sincere thanks and gratitude for allowing me such a special place in the ministry at Union. I am thankful to God that He has allowed us to work together in this part of the vineyard and I am excited about all He has in store for us together.

To all my special friends—and you know who you are—thank you for all the years of support, laughs and love you have given to me. I shall never forget all that you have done for me.

To my husband and pastor, the Rev. Dr. Sir Walter Lee Mack, Jr. You are my heart. I love, respect and honor you. Thank you for being my husband and thank you for allowing me to be your wife.

Finally, to all who will read this book I have written to share my story. I pray blessings to you on your journey to your wedding and, most importantly, your new marriage. Keep God first, keep family close and keep the devil off your guest list.

Kim Bush Mack

INTRODUCTION

Just a few days before I began writing this book, my life changed forever. I married the love of my life. Even now, it seems like it was a snapshot that I want to hold on to the rest of my life. Throughout the entire process of preparing for the event, our time was inundated with the details and organizing that go along with planning a wedding. Although I wanted my hair to look nice, my makeup to be correct, my dress and shoes to reflect distinction and honor, nothing could rival waiting to see the man that I had fallen in love with—now the man that would be the covering of my life for the rest of my life—at that altar. I must admit, I almost didn't see his face because by the time I got to the altar, tears flooded my eyes. I was excited about the day, but what I was most excited about was that I felt the Spirit of God upon me as I was about to make vows that would change my life forever.

I should not have been surprised that the Spirit of God would be upon me, my husband, and everyone gathered in the sanctuary, because from the very first moment we began planning our wedding, my husband and I decided and agreed collectively upon two things. First, we agreed that if no one else decided to show up at our wedding, it didn't matter as long as the Spirit did not forsake us at the altar. Second, we desired a wedding that would be a worship offering for our God and that relationships would not be destroyed in the process of planning the service. We both desired to plan a wedding where one person was for sure not to be on the guest list—the devil, the enemy, the trickster, the master of confusion and author of division. Yes, we decided that we wanted the Spirit of God there, and the devil would be nowhere on our guest list.

Now, you may be saying the enemy doesn't show up at weddings. Well, if you are looking for the devil to be in a nice bow tie with a cummerbund and patent leather shoes, you will miss the enemy. If you are looking for the enemy to be in a nice sequin dress that sparkles and shines at the glance of a light, you are missing the enemy. The enemy doesn't wait to show up at the wedding on the wedding day only, the enemy loves to distract and destroy things long before the wedding. He loves to get involved with the process, he loves to cause confusion among friends who have been friends for a lifetime. He loves to cause family to fight over who is going to ride in the limousine, who gets to walk down the aisle, or who gets the flower and who doesn't. He loves to upset the bride before she goes down the aisle, and even cause things to happen that will make the groom get cold feet before he says "I Do." Never forget what Jesus said about the enemy in John 10:10—he comes to kill, steal, and destroy.

I am writing this book because I am probably one of the few brides who can testify that I was able, with the help of God, to keep the devil off of my guest list. Yes, there were times when I saw him forming a weapon during the planning process of our wedding to use against me, but the one or two things that the enemy attempted to do never prospered, took us off focus, or even caused a moment of distress during the planning process of our wedding. So what happened? How did I get to be so blessed as to not experience some of the horrors that others experience while planning one of the biggest days of my life? While I know it was nothing but the grace of God that kept the enemy away, I also know that there were some practical things that my husband and I did to keep us on our job, while God was on His job. Therefore, I thought it would be most helpful to record some of this practical advice to share with other couples as they plan their weddings, for pastors, wedding directors, planners or just friends who desire to give advice to a couple on how to keep the devil off of your guest list.

One of the tactics that the devil uses to get on the guest list is to make particularly the bride, feel like this is the "biggest" day of her life. The gown she chooses will be the "most important" gown of her life, and if the activity of the day is not at "stellar level," he makes her believe the day will be a disaster. This is a trick of the enemy because, believe me, there will be more important days in your life than your wedding day. The day will come and go and life will happen immediately after. While the wedding day is a significant day, we must always remember that it is still a day that the Lord has made.

This book will reveal some of these kinds of anecdotes of spiritual insight that you must have to keep the devil off of your guest list. This book will also suggest some practical and "doable" things to ensure that your day is a blessed day. Now, I would like to warn you that if you read this book and even follow every step with detail, just know if you keep the devil off your guest list, the enemy is still shrewd enough to just sit in a window somewhere and watch. And if by chance he decides to slip in the back or sit on a window ledge somewhere, we have a remedy for that too, but you have to read the book discover what that is.

Now let's get to it—who is on your guest list?

THE PREPARATION OF THE GROOM BEFORE THE WEDDING

You have made a major decision in your life. You have now come to the place where you feel as if God is calling you to not only be responsible for yourself, but now you are called to be responsible for someone else—namely your soon-to-be wife. Therefore, because of the sacredness of the matter, it is important that you consider some tips about the preparation of a good groom/husband, before you prepare your guest list.

The Groom Is Called to Live a Life In Christ

The decision that you have made to be married is more than a mere announcement to the world that you are ready for matrimony, but it is also an announcement that you have matured to a place in your life that you are ready to put away some things that are in your past. Make no mistake about it, every man has a past. However, matrimony is calling you to put away your past filled with immature decisions, self-centeredness and perhaps even the tendency to be egotistical, because now God is graduating you to a life of responsibility, inter-dependence, and a place of great sacrifice. My husband, Sir Walter Mack, Jr., wrote a book entitled, *Passion for Your Kingdom Purpose*. In that book, he says, "Every man that is planning on making a contribution to the enhancement and the development of the Kingdom, must experience a season of detoxification. To speak of detoxification is to confront the reality of being cleansed, purified, neutralized, and revitalized from within. Detoxification is necessary because while we are meandering our way on this journey, from the crib to the grave there are many proposals, ideas, opportunities, influences, speculations, perspectives, and agendas that affect the way we see the world......because your manhood is affected by these conglomerates, it is important that you discover the things that have you intoxicated, and more importantly, what it is you need to do to enter into your season of detoxification." As it says in 2 Corinthians 5:17, "Therefore if any man be in Christ, he *is* a new creature: old things are passed away; behold, all things are become new."

In other words, announcing that you are ready for marriage is also an announcement that you are ready to walk away from the distractions in your past. Perhaps you were distracted by women, pornography, drinking, gambling, foul language, or even all forms of abuse. By all means, make up your mind that it is time for you to leave these demons behind you, and learn to embrace the invitation that God is extending to you to live a new life in Christ. If you are a man who already has it together, it is important that you still be careful that you do not fall into temptation and give way to the enemy having his way in your life.

Some questions to ponder as you prepare...

- Who are the people you must end communication with to focus on your marriage?

- What are some of the vices that you know you must walk away from in order to be a good husband?

- Why is your fiancé worth you leaving some things in your past?

The Groom Is Commissioned to Love

While it is a great thing for marriages to exist, it would be nice if all marriages could stand with the confirmation of love. It is interesting to me that in Ephesians 5:25, Christ commands the husband to love the wife, but he only tells the wife to submit. There is no greater feeling in the world than for a woman to be loved by a man, not to mention a man she is waiting to marry or has married. This process is not about the wedding only, this process is about you securing your love towards the one who will be your wife. To love her means that what is important to her will be important to you. To love her means that you will be willing to go to any length to make certain she is comfortable and safe. To love her means that you will allow her to access the secret places of your life and allow her to be a help meet to you. Love her, not so much with the material things -although it will help, but love her with your mind, body, and soul. I promise you, you will then have no problem with her submitting her life to you or giving in to your leadership, because she knows you love her.

Please do not confuse submitting with being submissive. To be submissive means that one does not have the ability to stand on their own. On the other hand, to submit means to give over to, or give in to. Love makes it so easy for women to submit, so I charge you as a man who is about to get married, practice loving "all" of who she is, and she will have her own way of letting you know she appreciates the way you love. David Levesque put love in the right place when he said, "You know you are in love when you see the world in her eyes, and her eyes everywhere in the world."

Some questions to ponder as you prepare…

- How do you like to show love?
- How does your fiancé/wife like for you to show affection?
- What changes do you need to make to show more love?

The Groom Is Encouraged to Know His Bride

During the planning process of my wedding, it was my fiancé/husband who made the process so much fun and so enjoyable for me. When we went to visit some of our vendors, I never really had to say much. Shortly after starting the discussion with our potential vendors, he knew if the conversation was one to continue or one to end by simply observing my non-verbal cues. This is so important because most of the time, the bride is on edge about all of the wedding details and plans. However, knowing your bride lets you know when it is time to "pray" and when it is time to "say". Most of the time we know what colors we want, we know what kind of cake we are looking for, we know who we want to do what. What is needed from you as a good groom is to know when we are at our limit, know when we are frustrated and when we are truly satisfied.

I once stated to my husband that if anything will test the strength of a relationship, planning a wedding will do just that. This is why knowing your bride is critical during the planning process. During this process, you will be forced to think together, work together, and plan together. Most of the time, the pace you set at this juncture will set a pattern for your marriage the rest of your life.

Because of the stress the wedding process can bring, it will be a good thing for you to plan a spontaneous one day trip, set up a spa retreat for your bride to relax, set times when you will talk about plans and times when you will not, send her flowers, and remind her that she is secured by your love. Knowing your bride requires attentiveness, patience, listening, compromise, and sacrifice. The best way to know her is to simply like her. Like who she is, and you will not having a problem knowing what she needs.

Some questions to ponder as you prepare…

- What are the things that you absolutely know about your fiancé?

- What are the things you want to know about your fiancé?

- What are some special things you can do for her during this process?

The Groom Is Called to Lead

The Bible has divinely set up the marriage establishment for the man to take the lead. What a wonderful privilege it is to have an anointing on your life in such a way that God calls you to take the lead. Taking the lead in the marriage and the wedding planning is not about a place of control and domination. But this is a calling to be a priest in the kingdom. I once heard my husband say, "Priestly function for men has to begin with the man taking authority and becoming a leader in the family, community, and in other areas of life…. It is mockery for a man to encourage his children to go to church, and he won't attend himself. It is impossible to lead your family and friends in prayer, when you are not praying yourself. It is impossible to preach and teach the necessity of investing and putting away for tomorrow when you are spending every dime you get your hand on. To be a priest is to lead by example in seeking the holiness and the righteousness of God for others."

Therefore, taking the lead requires being confident in who you are and who God is. While you are planning during this process, lead by initiating prayers, suggesting the necessity for reading God's Word, and taking time for worship and study. Do not be a groom that the bride has to beg to go to counseling, but be ready to whatever is going to make your marriage a solid entity. Take the lead in budgeting, paying the vendors, and making sure assignments are kept and understood with wedding participants. If you have a wedding planner, make sure she knows you just as well as she knows your bride. Taking the lead means being involved and letting your bride know that you care for her and you really do care about the wedding.

Some questions to ponder as you prepare…

- Have you sat down with your fiancé to discuss who will take the lead on what assignments?

- What are the areas of leadership in the relationship that you feel comfortable with and which assignments do you not?

- What are some changes you have to make in order to become an effective leader in your relationship?

PLAN BEFORE YOU PRONOUNCE

One of the things that I am most thankful that we did in the entire process of planning our wedding is that we decided to plan the details of our wedding before we officially announced our engagement to the world. While my husband planned an engagement proposal so unusual that the local newspaper did an article on the uniqueness of it, before there was a public engagement, there was a private one. I was indeed surprised about how the public engagement happened and when it happened. However, before he actually proposed publically, we had begun discussing some critical details about our wedding privately. This is similar to what God did in the life of David. Many of us know of David as the mighty warrior, the accomplished king, and the writer of inspirational psalms. However, before David became any of this publicly, he was anointed by Samuel in the middle of Jesse's field privately. Private adventures often bring much more excitement to public acknowledgements.

Your wedding announcement is going to attract so much attention. Depending on your dating situation, there will be some people who will be very excited about your announcement. Likewise, there may be some people who will not be so happy and will seek to cause drama from the time you announce your engagement until the time the wedding takes place. It is a natural thing for people who are connected to you, people who have walked with you during some very special moments in your life, and even some for tough times of your life, to invite their opinion into your wedding. Since these people have given you sound advice and wisdom in other areas of your life, certainly they would want to provide those same services during one of the biggest days of your life. This is a sure way for the devil to show up on your guest list.

Here is how it happens. By the time you have listened to what your mother and father want for your wedding that they didn't have for theirs, by the time you listen to both sides of the family about what is going to be a safe setup for the step parents and the divorced parents that are involved, once you entertain what date will work for people and what is most convenient for them but not you, after everybody has shared with you the location they would prefer, what colors you should have, how much money you should spend or not spend, by the time you hear all of these issues from other people, what is supposed to be a desirable entree for you and your fiance to enjoy, has now become a meal with all of these side dishes that you didn't order. One thing that I love about Jesus is that Jesus was always clear on His agenda and others either got with it or they didn't. I'm not suggesting that you shouldn't listen to wisdom, leave room for Godly advice or the opinions of people who care about you most, but what I am saying is that you have to have a plan, and let others know that the plan you have is one you really want them to respect.

To avoid inviting the enemy to your wedding, here are some things that you and the one that you are about to marry must decide before ever making your engagement public.

- How long will the engagement be?
- What is a good time for us to have the wedding, and does this allow adequate planning time?
- What will be our wedding budget?
- Where will the funds come from to pay for the wedding?
- What are our top three wedding location choices?
- What kind of reception do we desire to have?
- What will be the estimated number of people attending?
- What will be the wedding colors?
- What close family members or friends do we want to share our preliminary plans with before we make information public?
- How will we tell our family and friends?
- Who will do the counseling?
- Who will perform the ceremony?

Raising these questions is just the beginning of the process, and while most of these questions will not have definitive answers until later on in the process, by all means try to answer most of these questions with the person you are about to marry before making your announcement public.

Most brides leave the groom out of the planning stages of the wedding, however, my husband was involved from the very beginning. This afforded an opportunity for bonding that was unique and special in its own way. For example, when it came time for us to discuss the wedding photographer, we both desired great wedding pictures to preserve the memory of that day. One morning around 2 am, right over the telephone, we were up surfing the Internet for the "World's Greatest Wedding Photographer." We both knew we didn't have the budget to fly someone in from Spain or Italy, but thought it would be interesting to see what was out there. To our surprise, the 14th listing under "Greatest Wedding Photographer in the World" was in our own state less than an hour from our home—Mr. Shane Snider from Raleigh, North Carolina. We called, he answered, we met, and the deal was done. And to this day, we both rejoice over the fact that we, together, found the person who would preserve the memories of our day, and we were not disappointed. This is an example of team involvement that I believe can make a difference in your marriage later.

As the groom, it is important that you be a willing participant in the wedding planning process. What a woman needs more than anything is security. Your involvement can make her feel like you care and that you really want this. Be sensitive in this area and stay involved. Staying involved simply means that you ask questions, make suggestions, and are prepared to listen to discussions about the wedding almost every time the two of you talk. Just being receptive to your bride's excitement means more than you will ever know. The respect you give to your relationship now can majorly impact the marriage you will have later. It begins here during the planning process of your wedding.

If you are going to be a godly man in the home, the one who is answerable to God for the covering of the home, never forget that even though Eve was out of place in the garden, God asked Adam, "Where are you Adam?" Why wait until after the wedding to involve yourself in home affairs? I contend that the establishment of the home began when you asked her to marry you and she said "I will." While every man may not have the same interests in weddings that women often do, addressing these preliminary questions up front will let your bride know you respect her ideas, her opinions, her thoughts, and her role in the family.

Do you have to do everything together? Of course not. It is perfectly fine to delegate responsibilities among yourselves. The key is not who does what, the key is keep one another involved. When both of you are determined to stay involved, you will have a greater chance of keeping the devil off of your guest list.

THE GROOM SHOULDN'T LET THE RIGHT HAND KNOW WHAT THE LEFT HAND IS DOING

In Matthew 6:1-4, Jesus is charging the disciples to keep their ministry in perspective, and He reminds them that ministry is not about being ostentatious or showmanship driven, but there are times when what you do should be between you and God. The underlying message is that it is not always good that other people know what you know. In other words, some favored information is not for everybody, there are some things that you should keep to yourself.

Isn't it interesting that the wedding ring is placed on the left hand? Of course this custom dates back to the time when Archduke Maximilian of Hamburg, in 1477, engaged Mary of Burgundy with a diamond ring. When Maximilian gave Mary the ring, he placed the diamond ring on the left hand, on what is now commonly known as the wedding finger. It is believed that there is a vein in that finger that runs directly to the heart. He chose a diamond to place on her finger because it takes a diamond to cut a diamond.

When the ring is seen on the left hand, an instant message is already conveyed—you are engaged. That's why I urge ladies not to wear a ring on this finger unless it is an engagement ring because it is a good thing to protect the sacredness of that place on the left hand. While people who are close to you will know that you are engaged when they see the ring, it doesn't mean they deserve to know the details of your wedding day at this point. This is where you are going to need to pray for discernment because remember, once it is announced that you are engaged, everybody wants to insert their two cents into your planning process. So how do you manage this?

Identify the Voice of Your True Confidants

Even though you and your fiance have a plan together and you have a general idea of what you want for your wedding, it is important that you also have some true confidants as a part of your planning process who do not insert what they want for your wedding, but support what it is you desire. Their role is to just be a sounding board and tell you their honest opinion. For my wedding, we chose to share the pre-announced information plans with one of my sisters and one of his sisters. Not that we wanted to exclude our other siblings, but we used these two as sounding boards for the rest of the family, and to make certain that we were being realistic in our planning process.

After we shared information with our confidants, we were then ready to share with other family and friends. Not only did we share the plan with family and friends, but we also organized a planning team of selected individuals who we trusted to help us execute our plan. After you properly bring the right people on board to assist you, not only do you benefit from their help, but you are enlisting prayer warriors who will pray the enemy off of your guest list.

Identify Your "Frenemies"

There is a word that I believe is most valuable to understand during the planning of a wedding, and that word is "frenemies" A frenemy is an enemy in your life who poses as a friend. I hate to be the bearer of bad news, but during the planning of your wedding you will find out exactly who your friends are. You will discover that people you thought were your friends, weren't, and those that you thought were not your friends, you may discover that they were your friends all along. I had a friend who was planning a wedding and she wanted to use the knife set of one of her friends who had gotten married before. When she asked her friend if she could use the knife set, her friend said yes, but wanted her to pay a rental fee. This knocked my friend off of her feet, not to mention the rental fee she was assessed was almost as much as the cost of a new knife set. Yes, during the wedding planning, don't be surprised when even your friends use this opportunity to make money off of you. I am not suggesting that you should look to "free" your way through because wedding services cost, but what I am saying is that weddings have a way of revealing who people really are at heart.

Learn to discern these frenemies because these are also the ones who will call you for details of your wedding day, and then call up others and talk about how ridiculous and outlandish your plans sound. Don't let your right hand know what your left hand is doing. Pick your time and the people with whom you desire to share information. It's your wedding, not theirs, why should they be just as excited as you are?

Write the Vision and Make It Plain

During our wedding planning process, we had to plan for the anticipated participation of 3,000 guests and three receptions. Hence, it was critical that information be conveyed with the people we had entrusted to help us execute the plans of our wedding. We found it to be most helpful for us to write out our plan to share with our planning team, our family, and at the right time, our friends. Writing down what you desire on your day sends the signal to everybody you invite to assist you that you and your fiance have already thought through the process. This keeps your planning meeting from looking like a room shot up with a machine gun, but rather it will resemble a meeting with one target, one goal, one vision, one plan, and anything offered as a suggestion will simply add to what you and your fiancé have already prayed over and asked God to bless. If you desire to have a wedding planner, make sure they understand the vision that God has given you, and then invite them to use their methods to make your vision a reality.

Get Rid of Drama Channels

What I discovered is that drama does not have transportation and it will not show up on its own. Drama shows up with people. Therefore, to eliminate drama from your wedding plans, you must identify people who may bring drama into the process. During our wedding planning, we were very careful about who we asked to perform various tasks during the planning process. Even though a person may be a good friend to go out to lunch with you, this does not mean they can handle the pressure and all the changes that go along with planning a wedding. Be very selective as to who you will involve in your wedding planning because the wrong people may bring the wrong drama.

Here are some questions for you to ponder as you make your plans.

- As the groom, what is your vision for your wedding day?
- Who are three confidants you can count on to share your confidential plans?

- Who are the people you need to leave out of your early planning process for the sake of confidentiality and peace?

- What is your plan for handling drama with family, friends, your planning team, or your wedding director?

- What kind of support do you need from people who are closest to you as you plan your wedding?

MAKE RELATIONSHIPS A PRIORITY

Having been single for many years of my life, I have been requested to help plan practically all of my girlfriends' weddings. My sister and I were always so excited about participating in the planning and also directing these weddings. However, over the years, what I discovered is that many relationships are destroyed during the planning and the implementation of weddings. I have seen family members vow to never speak again, and friends have parted from one another over things as minor as the color of a dress, the style of shoes, what jewelry to wear and even who gets to ride in the limousine to the reception. It is in these tactical issues that the devil gets invited to the wedding.

During the planning of our wedding, the one thing that we were very clear about was that making and maintaining relationships had to be a deliberate effort. As you set your plans, things will happen that will aggravate you and even seek to destroy your peace. When this happens, remember that relationships are important. Even if you are negotiating with a vendor and you know they are trying to take advantage of you, guard yourself but never lose yourself because relationships are important.

When you are making your plans, there will be people you will be able to invite to assist and people you won't. It's not what is done that makes the difference in relationships, it's how things are done that makes the difference. To say this is one thing, but to actually do it is another. For example, when it came time for me to choose the vendor that would bake my wedding cake—for ladies this is a big deal—I interviewed several vendors, looked at various websites, and talked to people at wedding shows, because a major part of the wedding for me was how the cake would taste at the reception. I had chosen a company, until I talked to my eldest sister who was excited about a company near her hometown who had a reputation for baking the best cakes. Because it was important to my sister, I traveled 75 miles to see and at least talk to the company. When we arrived at the bakery, indeed I saw beautiful cakes, and the ones we tasted were even better than what they looked like. After tasting the cake and seeing the excitement on my sister's face, even though I had already determined who my cake caterer would be, immediately I made a shift. The taste of the cake could not outweigh the look of excitement I saw on my sister's face. In my mind, I said, *If she is this happy about me even coming to taste the cake, what would it do for her if I chose this cake?* Sure enough, when I told her I selected that cake, her eyes filled with tears because at that moment, she found her plank of contribution into my wedding. You don't know how this one move strengthened our relationship. Likewise, I would hate to think about how this one move could have hindered our relationship also. Yes I had my own plan for a cake, but part of my plan also was to maintain relationships.

Making Relationships a Priority Means She Can't Be Bridezilla and You Can't Be Groom Kong

It is interesting to me that one of the top rated reality shows is this show called *Bridezilla*. This show is popular because it highlights the irrational, over the top, emotional, and obnoxious attitudes that brides often have when planning their wedding. The question becomes, do you really have to be condescending, rude, and insulting to the people around you because you are getting married? My husband is a pastor and we have had conversations about the attitude shifts in some brides when they get engaged. For many of them, it seems that the world must stop because they are getting married. But the one thing that we must remember is that Bridezillas destroy relationships. On your special day, do you want to be remembered as Groom Kong or do you want to be revered as God's man during this process?

As people of God, we should use the wedding planning process to glorify God and minister to other relationships in the process. What an opportunity a groom has to show others that this day really is not about the couple, but it is about celebrating God for the miracle of relationships. You can have this kind of witness when you are patient and willing to seek understanding in all situations. Planning a wedding is a great time to encourage other singles to trust God and allow God to direct their destiny. During the time when all of the attention is on you, how impactful could it be for you to let people know that you are not the center of your joy, but God is the center and in all things, He should get the praise. For example, the night before our wedding, we had a worship service. After the preaching and praising, my husband unexpectedly gave me the mic to say a few words. When I took the mic, I began to beg the people for their prayers for the next day's worship service. Note that I didn't say "my wedding day," but the next day's worship service. The way to keep the devil off of your guest list is to make sure that worship of God takes place. If the devil shows up, he sure won't be comfortable sitting there. When you begin to see yourself as a ministry gift of God and not a Groom Kong, you will begin to impact relationships positively.

Making Relationships a Priority Means You Must Be Flexible

It is extremely important that flexibility be made a part of your plans for your wedding. Most people make plans for weddings that are not practical, not well thought out, and certainly without a back up plan. My husband who does pre-wedding counseling all the time asks one question of everyone he counsels concerning weddings, and he asked me the same question in the process of planning our wedding. He simply asked me, "What will you do if you are supposed to marry at 12:00 noon, and at 11:00, you hear of a threat of a hurricane that is supposed to hit at 11:30 am?" Do you pray that God will not allow the storm to happen, or do you put on your reservation card a space for email and texting information so you can provide last minute updates? Do you just let whatever happens happen, or do you, in advance, plan to secure a back up location and even secure your vendors for a back up date in the event a hurricane hits on your day? What do you do? Do you panic and lose control and allow disappointment and frustration to rob you of your occasion? Do you respond like this, or do you wait until the worst of the weather has passed and realize that who can make it, will make it and as long as the preacher and two witnesses are present, you can still exchange your vows with the truest of love and devotion to the one whom you will marry? Be flexible—it's really not the couple's day, it is the Lord's day.

Recently, my husband conducted one of the most fabulous weddings I have ever attended. While the setting was at a stellar level and the day was set for a most memorable moment, the devil sought to put himself on the guest list. Right before this outdoor wedding began, a decision was made to relocate all 250 guests from under one of the most elaborate tents I had ever seen, over to a garden area, because the structure of the tent had begun to give way. While the transition was swift and without much havoc, I immediately began to pray for the bride and the rest of the day. My husband who was to officiate the wedding, left my side to go check on the bride. When he returned, he had a smile on his face and I immediately asked how was the bride. He said the bride was fine, and that her perspective was clear that this day was all about God. The bride was a doctor, and when she was told that there was an emergency, she thought that she was going to have to take off her gown and do CPR on one of the guests. When she found out that it was a tent issue, she sighed and simply said, "I thought you all were talking about a real emergency." This bride represented the epitome of flexibility.

My husband, who has a tremendous sense of humor, during the ceremony, really flipped the entire experience. He used the moment to charge the bride and groom to learn from the tent experience. His first charge to the bride and the groom was to let this day teach you that a successful marriage must hold at its center the ability to be flexible. His second charge to the couple was to not allow any situation in their marriage to cave in before they act. The fabulous tent flooring had a caving section, which became the impetus for the move in the first place. He creatively used that situation to charge the couple to deal with issues before a cave in. Among other charges, this truly gave the day meaning and purpose. In both instances, we see flexibility. The couple was flexible enough to not allow this change to destroy their day, and the preacher was flexible enough to be able to use the experience as a point of application for the couple. One of the ways to keep the devil off of your guest list is to start your wedding day by telling yourself whatever happens, God has built you to be flexible.

Here are some ways the devil will seek to put himself on your guest list.

- Somebody's tuxedo or dress arrives and is too small or too large
- Members of the wedding party show up late or with the evidence of drinking alcohol the night before
- Rings are forgotten
- Wedding licenses are lost
- Florist gets lost trying to find the church
- Director is late to give directives to everyone else
- CD music is left behind or may skip during the singing of the song
- Family disagreements take place
- The three-year-old ring bearer cries the entire time while walking down the aisle
- The groom gets afraid to come into the church
- Someone stands and interrupts the wedding when asked, "Speak now or forever hold your peace"

These things can happen, but you must be convinced that nothing will steal your joy on this day. The old saints would say, "This joy I have, the world didn't give it to me and the world can't take it away." Being flexible means when stuff happens, you make adjustments, figure things out, and know that Romans 8:28 says that all things work together for the good of them that love the Lord and are called according to His purpose.

Let me leave you with one of my favorite sayings—Always leave room for life to happen.

Making Relationships a Priority Means Allowing People to Be Who They Are

One of the things that happens in the planning of a wedding is that things are processed from a very formal perspective. This is cool if your life is always formal and the people you involve yourself with are always formal. But the majority of people do not live a formal life always, therefore in the planning process of a formal occasion we have to transfer our focus from the informal to the formal. What I am trying to say is that you shouldn't expect people involved in your wedding party to just get formal and understand the importance of formality when they are accustomed to living very informal lives. Therefore, to keep from insulting their life and their intelligence, it is acceptable to give instructions on formal practices, but do this with kindness and patience.

Understand that patience is needed when people show up at the wedding late, a dress code is not followed, and RSVPs don't come in on time. Yes, some people know protocol, but not all do. So in regards to relationships, it is more important to maintain them and not allow formalities to destroy them.

I am not suggesting that formalities should be excluded from your planning, but just know that communication of the plans is important and whatever medium you choose to communicate your formalities, just make sure that it is always done with consideration of others and with a need to meet the people you know and love right where they are.

Here are some questions for the groom to ponder pertaining to relationships.

- What are you doing to establish a bond with your in-laws?

- How much time do you spend making sure your fiancé is in agreement with the wedding plans?

- Should people who arrive late not be allowed to enter the wedding or should another plan be considered?

- What ideas are you willing to incorporate from others and what are some areas in which you are absolutely not willing to compromise?

THE TRADITIONS REALLY MATTER IN ENGLAND

On April 29, 2011, an estimated two billion viewers watched what the generation would know as the "Royal Wedding of England." In the air of blissful love and affection, Prince William and Kate (Catherine) Middleton would exchange vows of love and commitment in an environment steeped in traditional pomp and circumstance. While most of the wedding celebration looked like it was custom planned for Prince William and Kate, the truth of the matter is that much of what the royal wedding showed us was pure tradition.

The wedding that William and Kate had was a wedding of tradition. In other words, they had no choice about some of the practices of their wedding—essentially they followed a script. Consider the traditions that William and Kate had no choice about following. We have endorsed many of these traditions that have nothing to do with God and the Church, they only have to do with England's tradition. Tradition only matters in England.

Traditionally, the royal bride wears a white wedding dress. This tradition originated with Queen Victoria in 1840. Another tradition concerns the wedding bouquet. When Queen Victoria married Prince Albert in 1840, she carried myrtle in her bouquet. After the wedding, Victoria planted a myrtle shrub in her garden at the Osborne House. Since that time, every British royal bride has carried a bouquet containing a sprig plucked from the same shrub. Traditionally, a royal bride leaves her bouquet in Westminster Abbey at the grave of the Unknown Warrior.

Beginning in 1923 with the Queen's late mother, all of the royal women's wedding bands have traditionally contained a portion of Welsh gold taken from the same nugget which was mined in Dolgellau, North Wales. This variety of gold is very valuable. While the original nugget is almost depleted, the Queen has since been presented with another large nugget for future wedding bands.

Most royal brides arrive to their wedding in a horse-drawn regal style carriage. Once the royal couple are married, traditionally they depart the ceremony in the same carriage. Even the music in royal weddings is dictated by tradition. Traditionally, royal weddings include the music of Mendelssohn's "Wedding March," the hymn "The Lord's My Shepherd," and Widor's Toccata from Organ Symphony No. 5.

Isn't it interesting that traditions often rule behaviors? Traditions are good because many of them honor the past, however, the challenge with traditions is that there are times when the practices may not be practical. For example, during the planning of our wedding, one of the things that my husband and I vowed to do was be more Spirit-led in our planning rather than tradition-led. We wanted worship, not tradition. We wanted freedom, not tradition. We wanted our feelings about things to drive the proceedings, not tradition. We wanted uniqueness, not tradition.

Consider some of the traditional things my husband and I chose not to do in our wedding.

We broke the tradition of one person giving the bride away.

I am the youngest of nine siblings and I have three brothers. Since my father has passed, it was important to me to have all three of my brothers escort me to the altar, each walking with me so far, then passing me off to the other. My oldest brother did the official giving away, along with my mother.

Keep the devil off of your guest list by allowing the Spirit to lead you to incorporate people who are significant and important to you.

We broke the tradition of an abundance of flowers and candles.

We were fortunate to marry in a very beautiful church facility, however, before being granted the privilege of using this facility, we had already determined that we were not going to invest our life savings in flowers, candles, ribbons, and banners. We had one candle signifying the passing of our fathers, and two standing flower sprays on the pulpit.

Keep the devil off of your guest list by not feeling pressured to spend a great deal of money on flowers that will eventually die and candles that will burn out.

We broke the tradition of a bride wearing the veil to cover her face.

I am a very open and transparent person and on my wedding day, I wanted to be free in the Spirit. Therefore, I didn't feel a need to cover my face because I didn't want anything standing between Him and me. It was good I didn't wear a veil, I contend that the Spirit moved freely because we were free.

Keep the devil off of your guest list by being free and comfortable with who you are and with what you desire.

We broke the tradition of having a traditional wedding ceremony.

The one thing that we prayed for during our ceremony was that people would come preparing to worship the Lord. Essentially, our wedding was a worship service with a wedding inserted throughout the service. Our wedding service involved praise teams, various pastors, video presentations, and a violinist accented with a liturgical dance. Youth celebrated our exit, lining the aisle with pom-poms.

Keep the devil off of your guest list by planning to worship God, rather than having people worship you on this day. Yes, it is your special day, but never forget it is the Lord's day first.

We broke the tradition of having just one reception.

We never desired to have more than one reception, however, because we wanted to accommodate as many people as possible and because of the limited space available at the hosting venues, we had to have three receptions. Two were held on Saturday for guests and special friends and one was held on Sunday for the members of the ministry.

Keep the devil off of your guest list by thinking about ways to incorporate your plan and do whatever you can to develop relationships.

We broke the tradition of having a large wedding party.

While we included many family and friends in our wedding, there were only two people who were actually a part of our wedding party—my sister and his brother. Elegance is often defined by simplicity.

Keep the devil off of your guest list by keeping it simple. There is nothing wrong with having many people be a part of your party, just remember that sometimes the more people, the more drama.

We broke the tradition of the program.

We did not use the standard wedding program with bells and flowers. We designed our own program with our pictures on the front that showed the passion we had in our faces for one another. A sample portion of our wedding program is presented in a later chapter, however the gist of our idea to have a non-traditional program was that we wanted something to represent us and to say the things that needed to be said like recognizing our parents, having letters of acknowledgement, explaining directives, and recognizing our vendors. Be creative, yet represent the royalty of our King.

Keep the devil off your guest list by making sure that your program recognizes people who are important to you. Also make sure all names are spelled correctly, and even consider a font that is fancy but legible.

DEMAND RESPECT FOR YOUR MONEY

One of the most trying experiences that we had planning our wedding was the selection of the company that would do our table settings for the reception. We were negotiating with the only business in our area that could handle a sit down dinner for 500 guests. This particular company knew that they were the only business that could seat that many guests, but because our wedding was a few months away, it didn't seem as if we were very high on their priority list. On three different occasions, they were supposed to provide a mock display of our table settings. After taking time away from our jobs and having our coordinators travel from their jobs to examine the displays with us, the tables were never set up and the only excuse we got was, "We have plenty of time before your wedding, and we will have to reschedule for you to come back to see the display." My husband had already lost patience after the second time this occurred, and after the third time, before he even got to the door, he puts his shades on his face and said, "This is it, find somebody else."

I knew the challenge of this task, but when I got home that evening, I went on the Internet and while surfing, I landed upon a website in Atlanta. Now we were in North Carolina, but I began to have a dialogue with this company in Atlanta. After one conversation with this business owner, I knew in my spirit that this was the right "soul connection". By the next day, this vendor had mailed out the swatches of cloths for me to see, she had already called the hotel for table information, she had already sent her quote, and by the next week, her airline ticket had already been confirmed. This vendor stated that she had never done a wedding in another state, but that she was sure she could make it happen. And she did in a major way. When that other vendor did not hear from us again, of course she was blowing up our cell phones. By that time it was too late. We had come to realize that our money demanded respect.

Regardless of who is paying for your wedding, it is important that you make vendors respect your money. A wedding can be quite expensive but if there is anything that I want to free people from, it is the pressure and the strain of thinking that a nice wedding requires spending a nice dollar. Never forget, the Word says that the love of money is the root of all evil. If you aren't careful, vendors will have your budget so out of control that it can cause stress for you and your fiancé, the family, and everyone involved when in fact, it does not have to. So here are some helpful ways to keep the devil off of your guest list as it pertains to budgeting and vendor needs.

Make Sure Your Plans Reflect Your Financial Ability

One of the ways to keep the devil off of your guest list is to start early in your planning process getting the money straight. A budget is so critical because it gives you an idea of what it is going to cost you to have your wedding, while also providing you the opportunity to plan with your financial ability in mind. You budget should be based on what is real, and not on what your dream was since you were 13 years old. Once you and your fiancé agree on a workable budget, make certain that you have considered where you are going to get the financing to foot the bill. Please be liberated from going broke to please people. Do what is necessary, but know that the two of you will have to live long after your wedding day.

Look for Alternatives if You Can't Find Exactly What You Want

If you are fond of watching reality wedding shows, you have discovered that creating a fantasy for your wedding is something that people really try to do. While there are many things from flowers to envelopes that will cost you greatly as you plan a wedding, never be embarrassed to shop for the best price, and even be willing to compromise what you have dreamed about to what is actually doable for your occasion.

The enemy will put you under pressure by speaking things through vendors like "this is your big day, go ahead and spend," "all eyes will be on you so you must spend this amount of money for this," "if your wedding is going to be royal, you have got to have this and that." It is interesting what people will tell you about your money when they are ready to take it from you. Make them respect your money. One of our vendors insisted that we spend $85 per table for our centerpieces, to have live flowers. We did not think live flowers were necessary at every table, so we quickly reduced that budget down to $35 per table. My husband insisted that we were not going to spend $400 on paper bands that would hold together our napkin and utensils. His simple reasoning was, "By the time people witness the wedding and get to the reception, they will be too hungry to even realize that we have a paper wrap holding our napkin together." I agreed and we told the vendor to scratch that.

Try to Pay for Things as You Go Along

There are many marriages that don't last beyond the date that the last payment was made on the credit card that paid for the wedding. By all means, if you have to borrow money to have your wedding, please spend conservatively. You do not want your marriage to be strained because of the expense of your wedding day. As a standard for integrity and Christian posture, try to have your wedding paid for the day you walk down the aisle, and if you owe after your wedding, follow your plan and pay off your debt. Keep the devil off of your guest list by making sure that everyone who is supposed to be paid for services such as directors, ministers, musicians, photographers, videographers, etc., is paid before your wedding day, or if they are to be paid on the day of the service, designate somebody to take care of this task so that this stress will not be placed upon you.

If you cannot pay while going along, by all means set a date and a plan for payoff and stick to it. Do not allow money to be a strain on your marriage.

Review All Contracts and Memorandums of Understanding

The Word tells us that in all of our getting, we should get understanding. While the enemy did not move during our wedding moment, he did try to raise his head afterwards. The hotel that hosted our guests and the place where we had our reception did not honor some of their contractual terms. During our planning, we sent a confirmed list of people whose hotel rooms we would pay for. Apparently, some of the desk workers did not get the official guest list and ended up charging unauthorized rooms to our account. Weeks after our wedding, we confronted the management about the matter and they indeed admitted that it was their error, but they insisted that we should still pay. We utterly refused to allow this five-star hotel to disrespect our money, so we retained a lawyer to handle the matter. By the time we turned in all of our written communication to our attorney, needless to say, the hotel had to eat the cost of these rooms because of their error. Make them respect your money.

If we did not have the written communication, it would have been our word against the word of the hotel, however, because we had our evidence in writing, it was obvious who was at fault. If you do not desire to retain a lawyer to read over contracts and agreements, make sure you take the time to get all pertinent details in writing and actually read what you are consenting to before you sign in agreement. A clear understanding may not keep the devil off of your guest list, but it will make sure that he knows you didn't make reservations for him, and you will put him out if he shows up.

Helpful Hints for Saving Money on Your Wedding

Choose a Wedding Date and Time that Is Less Expensive: The day and time that you choose to get married can drastically affect the cost. For example, weekday weddings are always less expensive, as are Sundays and Saturdays in November or January. These are times less likely to be used for weddings, and the venue would appreciate your business.

Monitor the Invitation Mania: A mistake is made when you buy for the number of guests and not the number of households. Buying for the number of guests can be impressive but expensive. If there are five people in the family, send the invitation to the household and let them respond accordingly. Remember, a nice quality presentation does not always mean expensive.

Find a Less Expensive Tuxedo Look: Many people will tell your bride that her dress is the most important dress she will ever wear in your life—well for me, it depends on how important your life is. There will certainly be other important days in your life. However, my message to you is if you can't afford a tuxedo, by all means get you a nice dark suit, and upgrade it with a black bow-tie. It's not the tuxedo that will make your day, it is the spirit you have while wearing it.

The Next Best Thing to a Live Band Is Recorded Music: Recorded music is a nice touch and not that expensive. Just make sure that the CD music is prepared in the order you desire it to play, and also clean dust from the CD and player to avoid music skipping. My advice to Christians is keep your music Christian, which will usher in the spirit of worship that you desire.

Pew and Chair Flowers: Flowers on pews and chairs are beautiful and show an effort of formality, however, you can skip this cost. Just make sure the ushers know where to seat your guests.

A Real Risk Bouquet: In a non-traditional wedding, you can do non-traditional things. If you do not desire a bouquet, try carrying a Bible, a candle, a fan, or even a fancy clutch or evening bag. Don't be afraid to take risks, this is your wedding.

Flowers Are Gorgeous: While flowers are gorgeous, they can be expensive. Consider using potted plants or silk flower arrangements that can be rented or used again. Hopefully, no one will touch your flowers on the altar to see if they are real or not.

What Is A Wedding Without Cake? I love desserts, and wedding cakes can be expensive. Therefore, feel free to choose alternative desserts like cookies, brownies, pies, cheesecake, or tarts. Try serving these with a butler passing by or as centerpieces on your tables. One table holding the desserts will also do.

Wedding Gifts For Your Guests: People who are excited for you really do not mind not receiving a wedding favor. Your guests are there to celebrate with you. Believe me, people will be fine with a simple thank you once the celebration has subsided. Save your money and don't spend much on wedding favors.

⊛ *Last Call for Alcohol:* Food and alcohol represent the biggest expense for most weddings. <u>A Christian should never promote alcohol at their wedding</u>. Remember, this is the Lord's day and not just your day. So it makes sense to cut back on that expense if you're planning a budget wedding. Broaden your idea of what a stylish and elegant wedding reception looks like and prepare to save. If your guests desire alcohol, hopefully they can afford their desire. Do not allow them to make their desire your expense. <u>Christians should demonstrate before the world that we can have fun without alcohol.</u>

Receptions: Brunch always costs much less than dinner. An abundance of fruit and vegetables can be just as appropriate as a steak dinner at a wedding. Fancy appetizers and non alcoholic cocktails add a touch of class to any reception. If you desire to have dinner, be wise and stay within your budget.

Dessert Reception: If you have a sweet tooth, this is the best way to indulge it! Serve nothing but sweets—wedding cake, petit fours, cheesecake, sundaes, and a chocolate fountain.

✳ *Cut Costs on Paper:* Take advantage of technology. Try communicating most information by e-mail. Today you can print invitations, response cards, and maps using web-based versions. Provide driving directions to the venue on your wedding website, issue save-the-date info and invitations via e-mail, and keep track of your guest count and meal requests via the Internet. Gather e-mail addresses or text numbers for last minute updates.

Think Local: Using caterers and florists who work with local producers can save you money.

⊛ *This Ring:* If you can't afford a four carat diamond ring, don't try to. The ring is a symbol of your love and commitment. Over time you can always upgrade to the standard of ring that you desire. Don't be ashamed to get something much less than you anticipated, and over time you can improve your ring status.

Budgeting for Your Wedding

There are many websites that can provide you with much information about planning a wedding budget, however we decided to use theknot.com as a practical guide for our wedding planning. I have chosen to provide a sample budget which you can also find on theknot.com that will give you a working idea of what it may cost for you to have a wedding. Please be mindful that this budget is for 150 guests. Your plan may be for more or less, so adjust these numbers accordingly.

Sample Budget

My Budget:	$30,000.00
Guests:	150
Female Attendants:	3
Male Attendants:	3

CEREMONY

Req.	Item	Our Estimate	Actual
✔	CEREMONY LOCATION FEE What affects price? If you're members of a congregation or you have a connection to a private site such as a country club, university, or relative's home, you may pay less than you would if you get married in a house of worship where you aren't members or you rent out a posh event space for the ceremony and reception. An auxilliary chapel may	300.00	

	cost less than the main sanctuary. Demand for the space can also affect cost.		
✔	**OFFICIANT FEE/DONATION** What affects price? Officiant fees vary widely. Some may charge $200 and up, others will charge nothing at all. Some ask for a donation to the house of worship; others may want simply to attend your reception. Popularity of the officiant can also determine the fee; if travel is involved, you may have to pick up the tab. Finally, some officiants charge more to attend the rehearsal.	300.00	▭
✔	**CEREMONY ACCESSORIES (CHUPPAH, CANDLES, ETC.)** What affects price? If you're using accessories such as a chuppah, unity candle, ring pillow, or flower girl basket, this is an area where you can spend a lot. Are you going all out with rose petals? Choosing bubbles for guests to blow post-ceremony? Decide what's important to you beforehand and whether you want to purchase or borrow things so you can stay within your budget.	180.00	▭
			subtotal 780.00

RECEPTION

Req.	Item	Our Estimate	Actual
✔	RECEPTION VENUE/RENTALS (TENT, TABLES, TOILETS, ETC.) What affects price? Costs fluctuate depending on time of year and day of the week (summertime and Saturday nights are more expensive, for instance). Popularity and location of the site are other variables that can raise the price, as well as whether yours is the only wedding at the site on that day. Renting a tent, tables, chairs, dinner service, portable toilets, and other amenities add big bucks to the total cost. Consider, too, the size of your guest list: more people = higher price. Remember to factor in tips for delivery people.	2400.00	
✔	FOOD & SERVICE What affects price? The size of your guest list and the menu you decide to offer are the number-one factors here. A dinner reception or seated luncheon costs more than than a cocktail party or champagne and cake reception. If you choose foods that are out of season (fresh berries, asparagus) or not local to your area (seafood, exotic game) you will also spend more. In addition, the type of waitservice can affect price. Remember to factor in tips for waitstaff.	60.00 x 150 guests (9000.00)	

☑	BEVERAGES & BARTENDER	16.00 x 150 guests (2400.00)	

What affects price? Top-shelf alcohol costs more than house brands (although sometimes these are the same). Serving beer and wine only is less expensive than offering mixed drinks. Having a limited bar, rather than an open bar, and limiting the kind of drinks offered will also cut down on bar costs. Having a minimum number of bartenders is another way to save. Remember to factor in tips for bartenders.

CHRISTIANS SHOULD STRONGLY CONSIDER NOT HAVING ALCOHOL AT THEIR WEDDING

☑	CAKE(S) & CUTTING FEE	750.00	

What affects price? Cakes are usually priced by the slice. Elaborate cakes with many tiers, custom designs, and handmade details cost more, as do fancy fillings and flavors. To save, some people buy an exquisite small cake to cut in front of guests and serve a sheet cake of the same flavor. There may be a cake-cutting fee at some reception sites (from $1.50-$6 a head) if you bring your own cake.

			subtotal 14550.00

49

ATTIRE

Req.	Item	Our Estimate	Actual
✔	**THE DRESS & ALTERATIONS** What affects price? Quality fabric, a custom design, and embellishments (beading, handmade lace) can all add to the cost of a gown. Alterations and rush orders also up the price. Explore your options. Need to save? Check out sample sales, look at white bridesmaid dresses, or borrow Mom's or a friend's gown.	1800.00	
✔	**HEADPIECE/VEIL** What affects price? Cost will increase the longer your veil, and whether it's handmade, crafted from lace or tulle, or has appliques will also affect the price. Headpieces vary widely; fine stones will obviously cost more than imitation jewels. Traditional headpiece not for you? Opt for fresh flowers or decorative hairpins.	300.00	
✔	**BRIDE'S ACCESSORIES (LINGERIE, SHOES, GLOVES, BAG, JEWELRY, ETC.)** What affects price? Exclusivity of the designer; materials (leather, satin, silk, and so on); whether you	300.00	

	already have some accessories, are willing to borrow them, or want all new ones.		
✔	**HAIR & MAKEUP** What affects price? Of course having your makeup done by a professional makeup artist costs more than doing it yourself. Demand and popularity of professionals you choose can also affect cost. Hairdressers will charge more depending on the complexity of the hairstyle you want; for instance, an updo costs more than getting a simple blowout. Remember to factor in tips for your hairdresser and makeup artist.	150.00	
✔	**PRE-WEDDING PAMPERING** What affects price? Decide how much pampering you're going to need — and make room in your budget for a special treat.	150.00	
✔	**GROOM'S TUX/SUIT** What affects price? Whether you rent or buy; exclusivity of designer; whether accessories like shirt, shoes, and cummerbund or vest are included in the basic rental; demand/popularity of the style you like.	180.00	

Req.	Item	Our Estimate	Actual
✔	GROOM'S ACCESSORIES (SHOES, TIE, CUFFLINKS, ETC.) What affects price? If you already own shoes, cuff links, studs, and other tux accessories, you might opt to use those. Or you may decide to go all out and get something special for your wedding day.	90.00	☐
			subtotal 2970.00

FLOWERS & DECORATIONS

Req.	Item	Our Estimate	Actual
✔	BRIDE'S BOUQUET What affects price? The types of flowers you choose and whether they are in season; the size and style of your bouquet (nosegay, cascade, and so on); the complexity of the arrangement; and whether a florist arranges it or you create your own will all affect the cost.	225.00	☐
✔	BRIDESMAID BOUQUETS (EACH) What affects price? The types of flowers you choose and whether they are in season; the size and style of the bouquets (nosegay, cascade, and so on); the complexity of the arrangements; and whether a florist arranges	100.00 x 3 people (300.00)	☐

them or you create your own will all affect the cost.

✔	GROOM & GROOMS-MEN BOUTONNIERES (EACH) What affects price? The types of flowers you choose and whether they are in season; the style and complexity of the boutonniere; and whether a florist arranges them or you create your own will all affect the cost.	15.00 x 4 people (60.00)	
✔	FLOWER GIRL'S FLOWERS What affects price? The types of flowers you choose and whether they are in season; the size and style of her arrangement (pomander or basket for example); and whether a florist arranges it or you create your own will all affect the cost.	45.00	
✔	ADDITIONAL BOUTONNIERES/ CORSAGES What affects price? The types of flowers you choose and whether they are in season; the style and complexity of the corsage or boutonniere; and whether a florist arranges them or you create your own will all affect the cost.	150.00	

✔	**RECEPTION DECORATIONS/ CENTERPIECES** What affects price? The type, size, and complexity of arrangements; the varieties of flowers and greenery used and whether they are in season; the number of tables that will have arrangements; and finally how many additional floral decorations (like floral arches, wreaths, and vines) based on the size of the room will all affect your final cost.	1200.00
✔	**CEREMONY SITE DECORATIONS** What affects price? The type, size, and complexity of decorations; the varieties of flowers and greenery used and whether they are in season; and how many additional floral arrangements (like arches, wreaths, and vines) based on the size of the ceremony site (altar decorations, pew arrangements, door wreaths and so on) will all affect your final cost.	420.00
		subtotal 2400.00

MUSIC

Req.	Item	Our Estimate	Actual
✔	CEREMONY MUSICIANS What affects price? Number of musicians; how long they play; whether they work for the ceremony site or you have to hire them; whether the same musicians will also play at your reception (you may get a price break). Professional musicians will cost more than amateurs or students. Remember to factor in tips where appropriate.	300.00	
✔	COCKTAIL HOUR MUSICIANS What affects price? Number of musicians; how long they play; whether the same musicians will also play at your reception (you may get a price break). Professional muscians will cost more than amateurs or students. Remember to factor in tips where appropriate.	300.00	
✔	RECEPTION BAND/DISC JOCKEY What affects price? Demand and popularity of the band or DJ can determine the price as well as how many people will play or emcee. How long you want them to play is	1800.00	

	another major factor. Professional musicians and DJs will cost more than amateurs or students. Sophistication of the DJ's equipment or the band's sound system can also affect cost. Remember to factor in tips where appropriate.		
			subtotal 2400.00

PHOTO & VIDEO

Req.	Item	Our Estimate	Actual
✔	PHOTOGRAPHER'S FEE What affects price? Demand and popularity of the photographer; whether assistants are required; how long you want the photographer to work; the number and types of cameras and other equipment; kinds of film; number and sizes of prints you buy (or the package you choose); photo treatments that mean extra darkroom work. Remember to factor in tips where appropriate.	1800.00	
✔	VIDEOGRAPHER'S FEE What affects price? Demand and popularity of the video-grapher; whether assistants are required; how long you	1500.00	

	want the videographer to work; the number and types of cameras and other equipment; length and type of the video and the number of tapes you buy (or the package you choose); special effects that mean extra editing-room work. Remember to factor in tips where appropriate.		
✔	ADDITIONAL PRINTS/VIDEOS What affects price? The package you purchase; how many prints you order; whether you want a bridal album and/or parent albums or additional copies of your video.	300.00	
			subtotal 3600.00

STATIONERY

Req.	Item	Our Estimate	Actual
✔	**INVITATIONS & REPLY CARDS (MAPS, OTHER INSERTS, CALLIGRAPHY COSTS, ETC.) (EACH)** What affects price? What kind of invitations you order; the type of paper they are printed on; the printing technique (engraved or thermographed, for instance); the number you need based on your guest list; whether you need extra enclosure cards, maps, or other inserts. Extra postage may be required depending on the weight and shape. How envelopes are addressed will also affect cost: professional calligraphy, laser printing, or addressing by hand.	5.00 x 150 guests (750.00)	
✔	**OTHER STATIONERY (ANNOUNCEMENTS, THANK YOU NOTES, ETC.)** What affects price? What kind of stationery you order; the type of paper; the printing technique (engraved or thermographed, for instance); how much you need; and whether you order along with your invitations. Extra postage may be required depending on the weight and shape.	150.00	
		subtotal 900.00	

WEDDING RINGS

Req.	Item	Our Estimate	Actual
✔	HER RING What affects price? The type of metal you choose (silver, gold, platinum); whether you have gemstones and or detailing on band; whether you opt for engraving; the size and weight of the ring; whether it is custom-designed or ready-to-wear.	300.00	
✔	HIS RING What affects price? The type of metal you choose (silver, gold, platinum); whether you have gemstones and or detailing on band; whether you opt for engraving; the size and weight of the ring; whether it is custom-designed or ready-to-wear.	300.00	
			subtotal 600.00

TRANSPORTATION & LODGING

Req.	Item	Our Estimate	Actual
✔	LIMO(S)/CAR RENTAL What affects price? Size, type, and color of cars; how many hours you rent the vehicles for; included amenities (champagne, TV, full bar, and so on); how many cars you rent. Remember to factor in tips for the drivers.	450.00	
✔	GUEST SHUTTLE/PARKING What affects price? The size of your guest list will determine how large of a shuttle/parking lot you need; how long you need the shuttle/guests need to park; whether you opt for valet service. Remember to factor in a tip for valet or shuttle drivers.	300.00	
✔	BRIDE/GROOM HOTEL ROOM(S) What affects price? Whether you rent a honeymoon suite at the same hotel where your wedding reception is held or where your guests are staying; the type of room that you book; additional amenities (room service, mini bar, and so on).	150.00	
		subtotal 900.00	

GIFTS

Req.	Item	Our Estimate	Actual
✔	ATTENDANT GIFTS (EACH) What affects price? Number of attendants you have in your wedding party and what you decide to give to each; whether you give honor attendants more expensive presents.	42.86 x (3 bridesmaids + 4 groomsmen) 300.00	
✔	FAVORS (EACH) What affects price? How many and what type of favors you give; whether you want personalization (your names and wedding date on them). Ordering in bulk can cut costs.	3.00 x 150 guests (450.00)	
✔	PARENT GIFTS What affects price? Number of sets of parents you have between you and what you decide to give to each.	150.00	
		subtotal 900.00	

MISCELLANEOUS

Req.	Item	Our Estimate	Actual
			subtotal

YOUR PERSONAL ADDITIONS

Item	Price
	subtotal

TOTAL COST OF WEDDING

	Total Spent	30.000.00
	Your Budget	30,000.00

Another option for budgeting may be to plan a budget by percentages. Please consider this format and use it accordingly.

Area	Estimated Cost	Actual Cost
Stationery items (3%)	$ _____	$ _____
Bridal attire (10%)	$ _____	$ _____
Reception (40%)	$ _____	$ _____
Flowers (8%)	$ _____	$ _____
Music (3%)	$ _____	$ _____
Photography (7%)	$ _____	$ _____
Gifts—attendants (2%)	$ _____	$ _____
Honeymoon (20%)	$ _____	$ _____
Misc. (e.g., special parties) (7%)	$ _____	$ _____
Total	$ _____	$ _____

(Read more about this at http://life.familyeducation.com/weddings/personal-finance/47409.html#ixzz1XApm5A3f)

Look Out for the Hidden Cost

Be sure you keep track of all your wedding expenses by saving all receipts and filing them in a safe place. Also, while you are planning, be mindful that the devil will try to get on your guest list by presenting hidden costs that you did not anticipate. Hidden costs won't catch you off guard if you plan for the following:

Wedding Band Equipment

Why It's Hidden: The cost of the wedding band includes fees for the musicians' time and the minimum amount of equipment needed. If your reception space is extra-large, then additional speakers and microphones could possibly be required to project the best sound quality.

The Cost: Anywhere from several hundred to several thousand dollars

How to Keep the Devil Off Your Guest List: Before booking your wedding band or DJ, you need to clearly explain the layout of the space (or have them check it out, if they're willing) so the vendors know exactly what they're working with. If they want to add in extra equipment, you should have them explain why it's necessary before you sign a contract or agree to pay for anything else.

Postage Stamps

Why It's Hidden: Stationers don't advertise the shipping costs of each invitation style; if they did, you might decide to go with simpler (read: cheaper) invites.

The Cost: Oversized, awkwardly shaped and bulky invitations will most often run you as much as $2 each to mail.

How to Keep the Devil Off Your Guest List: Skip the fancy boxed invitations and multilayer cards, which can bulk up quickly and cost a lot more than you bargained for.

Wedding Dress Alterations

Why It's Hidden: <u>Wedding dresses</u> are pretty pricey and stores don't want to scare away clients by listing alterations as part of the total cost.

The Cost: A simple hem can be less than $100, but completely rebuilding a bodice or moving zippers can send the price soaring.

How to Keep the Devil Off Your Guest List: Ask about what the store charges for every alteration you may need before you purchase the gown. If it's too much, don't be afraid to take your dress to a less expensive seamstress to have alterations done.

Photo/Video Overtime

Why It's Hidden: Your <u>wedding photographer and videographer</u> are booked for just a certain amount of time, so if your wedding runs a little longer than you expected, they'll charge overtime fees per hour.

The Cost: Starting at $250 per hour

How to Keep the Devil Off Your Guest List: When planning the day, factor in extra time for getting dressed and taking photos. You'll get a realistic sense of how long everything should take. Refer to this itinerary when booking your photo/video vendors.

Welcome-Bag Delivery

Why It's Hidden: Most hotels don't factor in a welcome-bag delivery fee when you reserve a block of rooms. They may fail to mention the rate unless you ask—they'll just add it to your final bill. Inquire about this up front. They may even charge you a fee for holding the welcome bags if you drop them off before the guests arrive.

The Cost: Up to $7 per bag

How to Keep the Devil Off Your Guest List: During the booking process, ask about the hotel's policy on receiving and delivering welcome bags to guests' rooms. It may be free or cheaper if they hand the bags out at the counter as guests check in. If you don't want the extra charge, you can distribute welcome bags at the rehearsal dinner.

Rental Transport

Why It's Hidden: You'd assume that the rental companies would include these extra transportation fees in the per-item costs (do they honestly think you're going to fit 150 chiavari chairs in your own car?), but surprisingly, they don't.

The Cost: From $50 up to more than $500

How to Keep the Devil Off Your Guest List: Ask the rental company what their shipping and packaging fees are up front—if the cost is too high for your budget, shop around a bit. You just might find that you'll actually save some money by renting items from a more expensive company that includes delivery costs at no extra charge.

Taxes

Why It's Hidden: Even though these aren't exactly hidden costs—we all know that there are taxes on almost everything—most couples don't think about how much they'll end up owing during the planning process.

The Cost: This will depend on the total amount of money you're spending as well as the location of the event (taxes vary in different areas).

How to Keep the Devil Off Your Guest List: There's no getting around paying taxes, but paying the entire bill in one lump sum can help lower the overall price, especially in the winter when vendors have fewer weddings to cover their bills.

Cake-Cutting Fee

Why It's Hidden: If you use the cake provided by your reception site, the charge is typically wrapped into the cost. Going with an outside baker can jack up the price. Why? Because your venue's workers are responsible for slicing and serving each piece, then cleaning the dishes. This means more work for their staff.

The Cost: From $2 to $5 per guest

How to Keep the Devil Off Your Guest List: Go with the site's cake baker. Don't worry: They'll likely be able to work with your vision. If you're set on a particular cake baker, then call your venue and find out what the fee is before you sign a contract.

Coat Check

Why It's Hidden: When you book your venue in the summer, it's easy to forget just how cold it'll be in winter months like December.

The Cost: The damage starts at around $200

How to Keep the Devil Off Your Guest List: Union rules may dictate the number of people who are required to work the coat check (and the amount they get paid). Have a good approximation of your total guest count when you book the coat checkers.

Gratuities

Why Its Hidden: Many couples often think that the "service charge" is a tip for the event staff when it's actually an additional fee that the catering halls charge. For what? To cover their own cost for hiring servers.

The Cost: Typically 15 to 20 percent of the event's total food and drink fee

How to Keep the Devil Off Your Guest List: Once you get the proposed fee, add the service charge percentage so it's already accounted for before the event. The last thing you want is to get hit with an unexpectedly huge bill that just about breaks the bank.

(You can read more about this subject at <u>Wedding Budget: 10 Hidden Wedding Costs—Wedding Planning—Wedding Budget—TheKnot.com</u> <u>http://wedding.theknot.com/wedding-planning/wedding-budget/articles/10-hidden-wedding-costs.aspx#ixzz1XAmjZYF2.</u>)

WHEN YOUR WEDDING BECOMES WORSHIP

During our wedding, the one thing that we desired more than anything was for worship of our King to happen. Because my husband is a pastor, it was important for both of us to have our wedding honor God in worship as we exchanged vows of love and devotion with one another and our God.

Our wedding had become the buzz talk of our region. This was not of our desire, but this was the result of so many people being excited for us. As a result, the rumor had circulated that this was going to be the royal wedding of the year. What I shared with my husband was that it was not possible for us to live up to that standard, considering that the "royal wedding" that they had in mind was one of materials and commodities. Our focus was simply to glorify God and have a wedding that would invite worship. Therefore we put the following letter in our wedding program to set the tone for our intentions:

Greetings…..In the name of our Lord and Savior Jesus Christ! We are so excited that you have joined us for our special moment of sharing vows of love, affection, and dedication to one another.

It is said that Archduke Maximilian of Hamburg in 1477 engaged Mary of Burgundy with a diamond ring. When Maximilian gave Mary the ring, he placed the diamond ring on what is commonly known as the wedding finger. It is believed that there is a vein in that finger that runs directly to the heart. He chose a diamond to place on her finger because it takes a diamond to cut a diamond.

You are here today because we both are convinced that God has called us to be the diamond uniquely designed to cut into each other's heart, thoughts, feelings, and desires. Therefore on this day, as you will hear vows of faith and love, and witness us exchange rings of commitment, we welcome you to join us in this celebratory moment of praising God and giving Him the honor for the things that He has done. It is our desire that this ceremony today will seal our intent to be accountable to God, our church, our family, our community, and of course to one another.

From the early planning stages of this wedding, we both desired that this wedding would be about building relationships and not destroying them which often happens during weddings. Therefore, we have sought to find ways to make your experience and time today with us as pleasurable as possible. We could not have done this without the help of a host of friends and family. We are thankful for the assistance and encouragement of the Union Baptist Church Family, and we appreciate the St. Peters Church Family for opening their doors to us.

Many have compared this wedding to the "royal wedding of England". However, it is not our intent that this wedding be "royal" because of commodities or material investments, but that it stands as a "royal wedding" because of a "royal King" who saved us and cleansed us with His blood. Not only that, but we deem this to be a "royal wedding" because we have "royal people" like you in our lives, sharing this special moment with us.

Again, thank you family and friends for being here today, and continue to pray for us as we embark upon our Union together.

> *Because of the Resurrection,*
> *Sir Walter Mack and Kim Romaine Bush*

When we set the atmosphere straight with this kind of stand, focusing on the royalty of our King and the royal people sharing the special day with us, I believe it gave God a channel to enter in such a way that the main focus would not be my dress, earrings, shoes, flowers, candles, VIP's, or anything superficial, but we did our very best to prepare the way for God to come through, and God did, and worship happened.

"Wedding" is a word that should be synonymous to worship. A Christian wedding should always leave room for God to show and demonstrate His power and authority. I believe that D.A. Carson described worship in a wedding setting in a unique way when he said, "Biblical worship is God's covenant people recognizing, reveling in, and responding rightly to the glory of God in Christ in the power of the Holy Spirit." David Peterson unpacks it this way when he declared that, "Worship of the living and true God is essentially an engagement with Him on the terms that He proposes and in His own time it is God who makes the marriage possible." What these writers are essentially saying is that worship is simply letting God control what happens in the moment, while submitting our will to God's desires.

Worship in a wedding can happen, but worship must be the intent of the service and then a wedding somehow finds its way in there somewhere. When a Christian wedding is planned, the feature of the day is not the bride, it's not the groom, it's not the flowers, it's not the candles, it is the presence of God being there. This is what makes your wedding royal—when God shows up.

With our wedding, we attempted to have a worship order and structure that was well thought out and carefully planned. We did not want a ceremony that had rituals without meaning, but rather we desired an experience that would mean something to us, and everybody connected to us. Therefore, we used the following worship order that we believed represented the royalty of the Christ whom we honor.

Praise and Worship Service—The Praise and Worship music should charge the atmosphere while guest are seated and the entrance of families and friends are made. The choir music was accented by a liturgical dance presentation which really set the tone for worship.

Call to Worship—A worship leader led the worship ceremony and interjected throughout the wedding where necessary.

Invocation—This prayer was led by a guest pastor and it centered on the importance of God being among us, and the people being open to invite God in.

Hymn of Praise—The hymn of praise that we selected was "All Hail the Power." The congregational hymn is so significant because it allows the people to participate and really highlights that God's presence is among us.

Scripture and Prayer—These parts of the service should reflect humility and celebration for the hour. The Word is full of love scriptures and they are most appropriate to use for this kind of worship.

The Occasion—The occasion is a theological exposition given in the way of a five minute sermonette that will define for your guests why we are here. This is a good time to get people engaged and make the connection theologically between God and the purpose of love.

Song Selection—The songs for a Christian wedding should reflect Christianity. It is acceptable to use nice loving secular songs, however, if you desire worship to happen, seek to use music that reflects God and motivates your guests to worship. The entrance of the Groom and the Bride was set to music that expressed our faith and our story.

The Ceremony—By all means, this is the highlight of the exchange of vows and devotion to one another. Make sure that you explain to the minister your desires for vows, however, let the minister guide you at this point. A Christian wedding should reflect Christian vows.

Holy Communion—Holy communion was taken by all guests who attended. Communion was passed out as people entered the sanctuary and at this time in the worship, we corporately celebrated the body of Christ. This was a very sacred moment, and a way to honor our salvation publicly.

Charges—This particular part of the service is optional. However, we included ministers who gave a charge to the church, to our family, and to each other. These charges lasted about 5 minutes each, and it really kept the wedding focused on the purpose of marriage as seen in the eyes of God.

Video Presentations—Video presentations during your wedding can be very appealing. They add a contemporary flare, while bringing your wedding celebration into the present age. If you are going to use this medium, please make sure that everything is professionally recorded and presented with excellence. We used the video to show our engagement pictures and a poem read by Dr. Maya Angelou.

The Violinist—Violins are very romantic in this setting. We were able to contract a Christian violinist who provided a crescendo to all that had preceded. Again, seek to keep your music worshipful, and worship will happen.

Pronouncement and Recessional—Once you are pronounced as man and wife to the people, it is fine for you as a Christian to show intimate affection with a kiss and a hug. People should feel your passion for one another, but save some for the honeymoon. We decided to add energy to our recessional by having 200 of the youth in our church line the aisles as we went out of the church with balloons, noisemakers, and pom-poms. This was so much fun, and the youth also reminded us to have childlike faith in God for our future.

Important Factors for Planning Worship

All wedding activities must be preceded by prayer and supplication.

Choose a place where the environment is conducive for worship. Most of the time, a sanctuary fosters this more so than an outdoor setting, beachside setting, convention hall, or at the Justice of the Peace.

Make sure that your worship participants understand their role and please remind them that for a wedding, there is excellence in brevity.

It is ok to be creative in your approach and have a sermon during your ceremony, communion, liturgical dancing, worship through instruments, and even a word of wisdom from couples married 50 years or longer. While this is creative, it also must be done in decency and in order.

Make sure that the sound system is functioning well, and if there is to be recorded music played, please work with the sound operator to know the exact cues. Have live musicians ready to play in the event that the CD skips.

It is important that your rehearsal moments start on time, participants be present, and that people understand the discipline that is needed for worship to happen.

Inform all wedding participants that in a Christian wedding, there should be no alcohol hangover for the wedding day and that the worship should be preceded by prayer with all wedding participants.

For the ease of seating, the ushers must understand the seating arrangement. Because this is a worship service, you do not have to follow the protocol that nobody can come in after the bride. Give consideration for those who may be late for any given reason and allow for seating to take place in the back of the church if anyone comes in late.

Directors of weddings should have some experience at directing, understand how to do several things at a given moment, be able to work with people under pressure, and know the importance of respecting the Spirit of God during the wedding celebration.

Emphasize that the wedding is worship to all participants and guests and invite them to allow the Spirit to move them while also respecting the order of the day. Dress attire should be modest, no distractive jewelry that does not represent class or the kingdom should be worn. No sunglasses, chewing gum, men with earrings, intoxication, or sexually explicit music should ever be a part of a Christian wedding.

Make directives after the wedding very clear so that the guests will have a good idea of your expectations for the day. It is ok to announce in a printed format where gifts may be placed and that monetary honors are also welcomed. While this information should be listed in your invitation, it is a good idea to remind the guests on your wedding program.

10 PRACTICAL STEPS FOR A GROOM PLANNING HIS WEDDING DAY

1. The groom should make the engagement and the announcement one the bride will never forget. It is a special moment and special moments demand special consideration.

2. The groom should be prayerful about the decision to marry and as soon as possible, get into pre-marital counseling to discuss matters such as communication, personality differences, expectations, sex, finances, family planning, etc.

3. The groom should initiate the planning of the wedding and discuss ideas with the bride before inviting others' opinions about your wedding day. The groom should show excitement and enthusiasm about the miracle that God is performing through the celebration of marriage.

4. The groom should assist in securing wedding and reception locations as soon as possible and be flexible with the dates that you are requesting. You are not the only man who is desiring to be married to a lovely bride.

5. The groom should seek to alleviate any drama from the life of the bride. There will be enough pressure for her to contend with so it would be helpful if the groom provided a time for relaxation, a spa treatment, a dinner or a movie during the wedding planning process.

6. The groom should establish an affordable budget and eradicate the feeling of guilt when you can't afford something you really desire. The wedding is one day and you must live the next day. If parents are involved in financing the wedding, the groom should take the lead in the discussion on cost. I know traditionally it is the responsibility of the bride's father, however, it will speak well if the groom will man-up and engage in discussions with the father as well.

7. The groom, along with the bride, should inform family and friends of the wedding plans in a written format or by email so that the devil won't put himself on your guest list by confusing your information.

8. The groom, along with the bride, should request a face-to-face meeting with all of your vendors in unison so that coordination can happen among them. This is a good time for them to build a team before your day occurs so that they can work together for the success of your event.

When meeting with the groomsmen, please inform them that drinking and hangovers will not be a part of the worship experience of your wedding.

9. The groom should assist the bride in making certain that all invitations are mailed out on time. Please include a place on your response card for email addresses or another way that you may contact people for last minute notifications.

10. The groom should plan for the unexpected, plan for the unexpected, plan for the unexpected..........And Keep the Devil Off of Your Guest List!